Acknowledgements:

Endeavour, Newfound Notes was written, devised and completed with the support of a 'Time to Write' Northern Writer's Award facilitated by New Writing North and funded by the Northern Rock Foundation.

The development of the poem into physical theatre and accompanying music has been funded by Arts Council England, North East.

Biscuit Publishing thanks:

ACE North East for providing additional funding to assist this publication. Many thanks to Three Over Eden and Gobble Racket for their interest in the piece and their ongoing creative input.

"The world will hardly admit of an excuse for a man leaving a Coast unexplored he has once discover'd, if dangers are his excuse he is then charged with Timorousness and want of Perserverance and at once pronounced the unfittest man in the world to be employ'd as a discoverer: if on the other hand he boldly incounteres all the dangers and obstacles he meets and is unfortunate enough not to succeed he is then charged with Temerity and want of conduct. The former of these aspersions cannot with Justice be laid to my charge and if I am fortunate enough to surmount all the dangers we may meet the latter will never be brought in question. I must own I have ingaged more among the islands and shoals upon this coast than may be thought with prudence I ought to have done with a single ship and every other thing considered, but if I had not we should not have been able to give any better account of one half of it than if we had never seen it, that is we should not have been able to say whether it consisted of main land or islands and as to its produce, we must have been totally ignorant of as being inseparable with the other."

Captain James Cook
Fri 17th August 1770

Endeavour

(Newfound Notes)

earest,
they're saying this be
the greatest seafaring voyage
of discovery ever attempted.

Ah say it's a mad-fool errand
if ever there was one.
A slow slide round the globe
to chart the transit of Venus.

We seek an elusive goddess, Dearest.
Hail Mary, Mother of our Lord.

The great ship that left England
has shrunk to the size of a thimble.
Riding ocean currents, white crests
where dolphins tumble.

We crossed the line. I was stripped, shaved
and dunked three times in the Little Christ
watched his temper burn under steaming skies
into monsoon screams and there were solid waters
Dear, towering in the curtain play of polar lights.

And we, Captain and Crew
not one of us can sleep
since we are all spellbound
by the glare of the Southern Cross.

Cook keeps us alive with his wild newfangled notions:

cauldrons smoking down below
shifting rats and plagues of lice
he insists on airing linen, set rigid instructions
on how to wash, as if we're suckling babes.

We gnaw cabbage every other day.
The butcher serves fresh meat.
Each man onboard wears a jacket
of finely woven 'fearnaught'
and drinks a brew of white rum and beer.

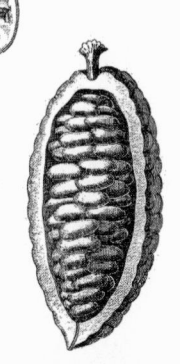

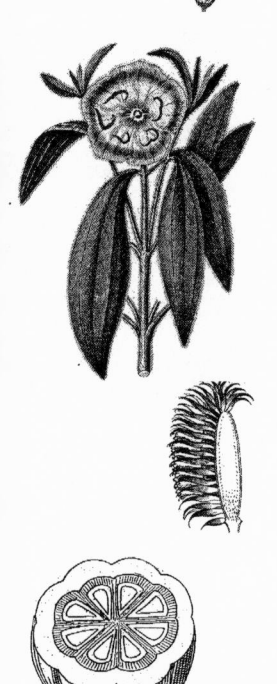

The old sailmaker, Ravenhill's hardly ever sober.
He has a gobfull of gallows tales of the flux and the gripes;
of sailing the Pacific with Anson's privateers.

I've heard him wailing hornpipes, odd nights
and clambering with a horn lantern, collecting
stars that get snagged in the rigging.
We all binge on fruit whenever we land.
Breadfruit, banana, coconut, kiwi.
The names alone'd make you judder.

We are so far out from any shore
that earth and rock and soil
shift in my memory
with no more substance than wood smoke.

Ye can walk on it, surely not?

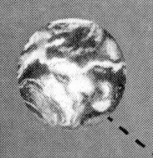

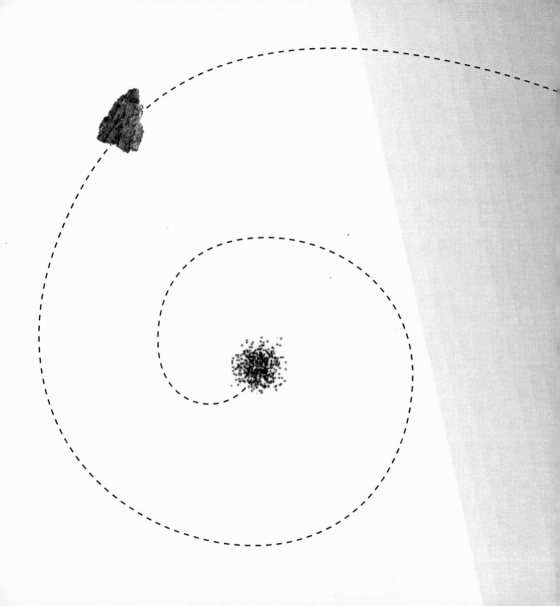

The drink today is a drum skin
  pulled tight over a dried-out gourd
    we wait for a storm god to beat it.
      Nothing comes as nothing's come
        since the sea became a carcase.

        We sit, scrub decks, darn canvass
          make scrimshaws or else stare blind
            at the world's rim, watch cats paws ripple
              shadows pass. We carve new prayers for wind.

          Instead we get an obese moon
            low enough to snag its arse on the mainsail.
            Spring a leak, spill its load all over the ship
            and threaten to take us down.

          The moon here wears lampblack tattoos
            of ill drawn men, circles, birds, crescents, stars
          whorling bands of calms and currents.

        I drop shells I've scratched with wishes
          into the crystal deep, surprised to see them sink.

      I lost another yellowed tooth today.
    I keep it in my pocket. I hold it up to the tattooed moon
compare their scripture to suss the trick of longitude.

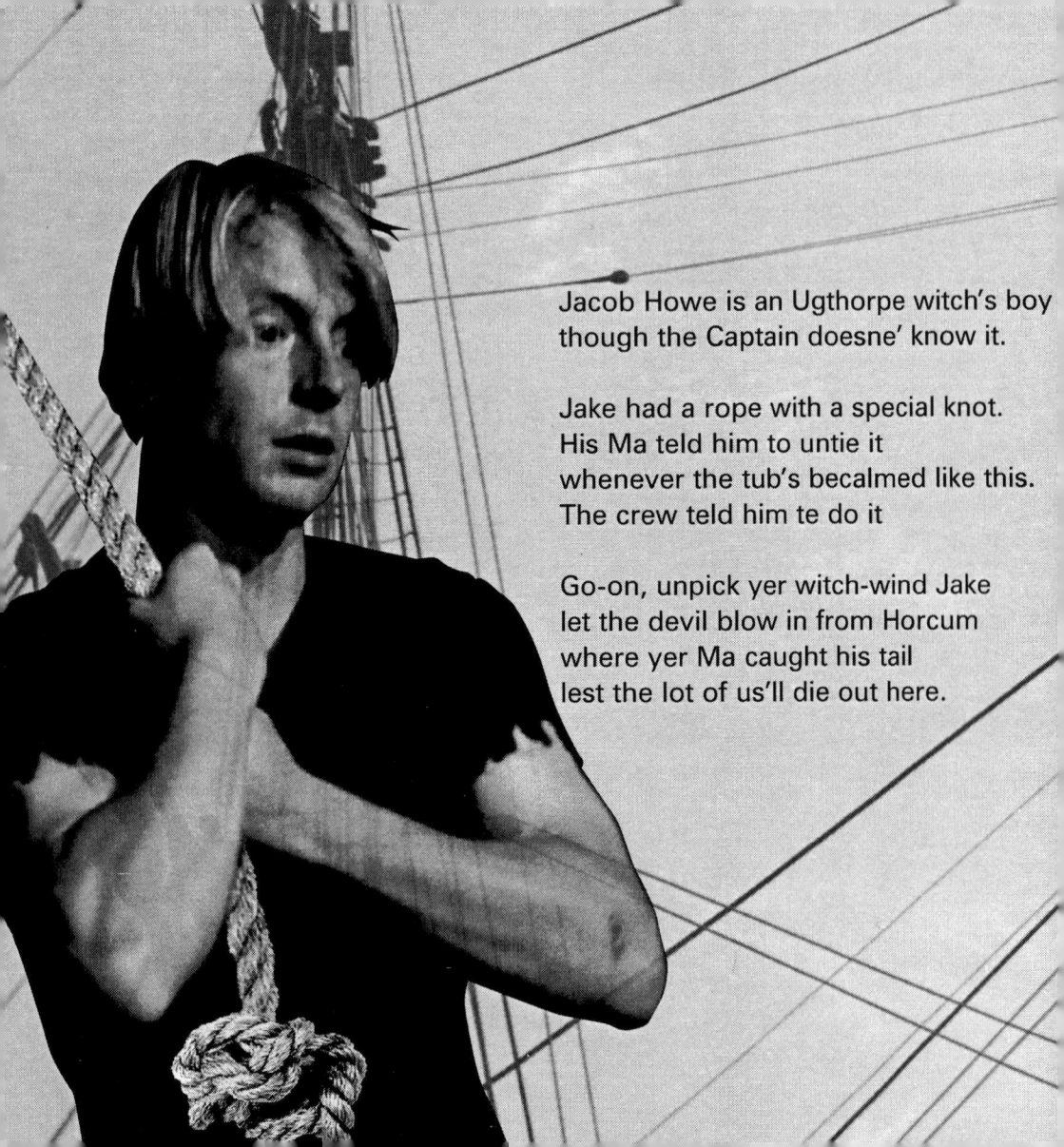

Jacob Howe is an Ugthorpe witch's boy
though the Captain doesne' know it.

Jake had a rope with a special knot.
His Ma told him to untie it
whenever the tub's becalmed like this.
The crew teld him te do it

Go-on, unpick yer witch-wind Jake
let the devil blow in from Horcum
where yer Ma caught his tail
lest the lot of us'll die out here.

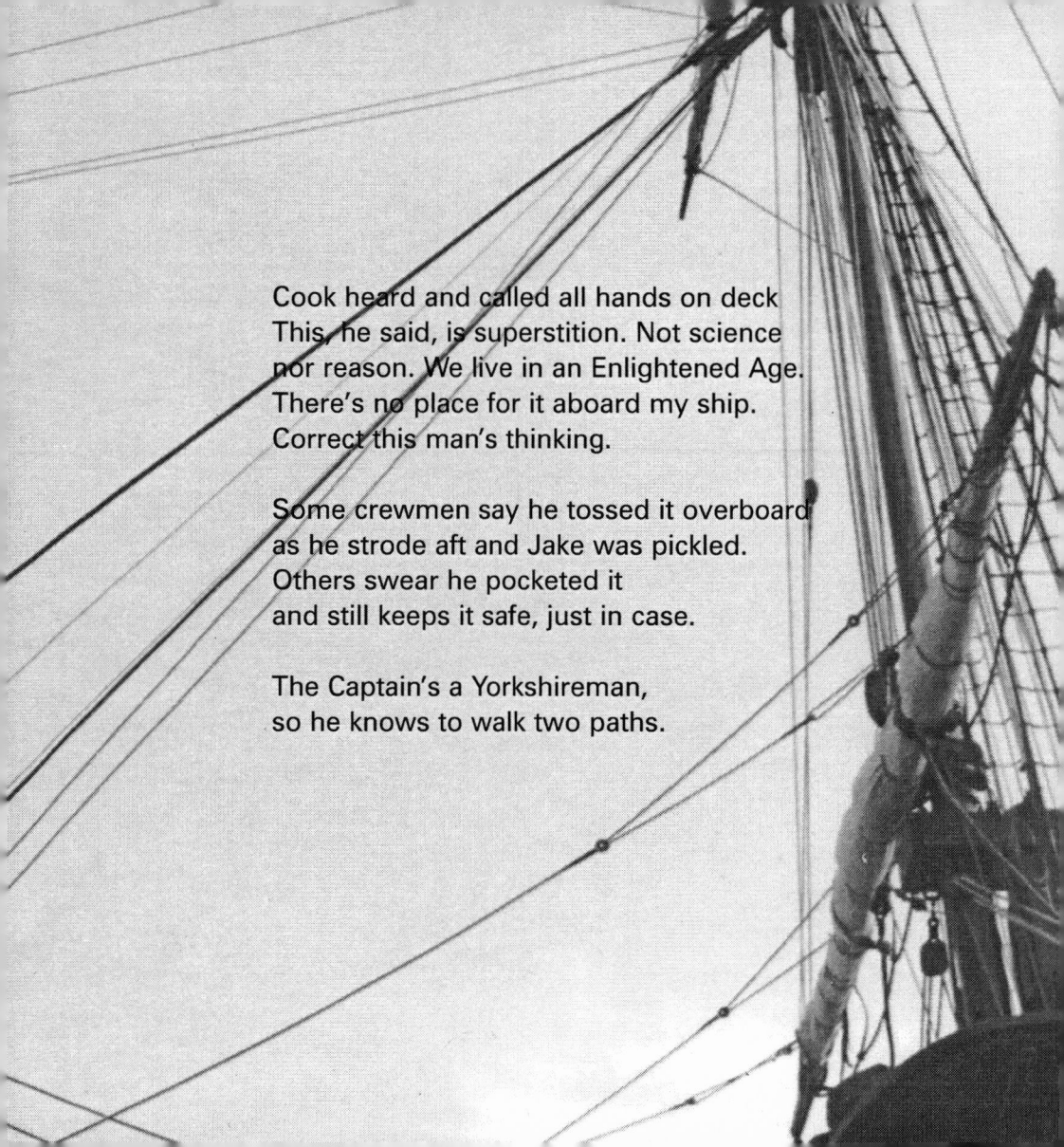

Cook heard and called all hands on deck
This, he said, is superstition. Not science
nor reason. We live in an Enlightened Age.
There's no place for it aboard my ship.
Correct this man's thinking.

Some crewmen say he tossed it overboard
as he strode aft and Jake was pickled.
Others swear he pocketed it
and still keeps it safe, just in case.

The Captain's a Yorkshireman,
so he knows to walk two paths.

Everyone's dreaming of O'taheiti,
the bounty, the plenty
everything's perpetual flowering.

The Priestess Oberea and her train
of handmaidens. The warring island chieftains.
The Arreoy's lap dance and the thieves of Eden.
The two pollen-angels that joined our expedition.

The lurid juice of the Ripe Land;
for which the butcher was flogged with the cat-o-nine-tails
as the royal guests toured the ship, bringing strings
of black pearls and a Green Bough for friendship.

They seemed upset at our way of a greeting.
It could be the manner in which he was whimpering
though in paradise they practice human sacrifice
and wring the necks of unwanted babes.

We tested our weapons on their scimpy atolls.
Tasted our fill of free will and taboo. Now the ocean
recasts a mirage of an island long since passed.

The livestock we obtained are unused to European grain.
The hogs, goats and poultry have died.

Tupia is teaching our sailmaker
to wail Tahitian temple songs.
The fruit stocks have begun to shrivel
and our memories are bruising to the touch.

The shock of tropical plumage
draws silent awe as it settles on the mizzen
black on red with a cutlass for a bill.

Prunes itself then takes off
trailing its shadow over our dampened planks
skimming the empty steppes of space.

Next day, Nicholas Young hails a pack of seals
bobbing asleep on the surface;
then, the merest smudge of land at last.

Unreal fronds of cloud that wrap
A range of mountain peaks. On the breeze
a smell, I've not smelled for weeks.

All hands grip the rails. All eyes are slits
against the glare, 'cept Cook's who closes one
threads the other through a lens, aims it at the shore.

I watch a bead of sweat run down his cheek
and wonder if he knows where on earth we are.

Mr Hicks mutters, 'Terra Australis Incognita?'
The Captain shrugs and orders a sounding.

We bring civilization.
  Gifts from the last place we landed.
    We bring sovereignty and the British Itch.
    The Good King's English, though
      George be German born and bred.

      We bring culture to the noble savage.
      Logic, the reason of the Godfearing man.
      Excuse me while I scratch my bites
      while I chew the weevils in my bread.

    From the beach a crest of war canoes
      raising a shanty that sweeps aside the waves.
    Drumming as they pass with the flat of their paddles
  swarming, slicing, stoking up the sea.

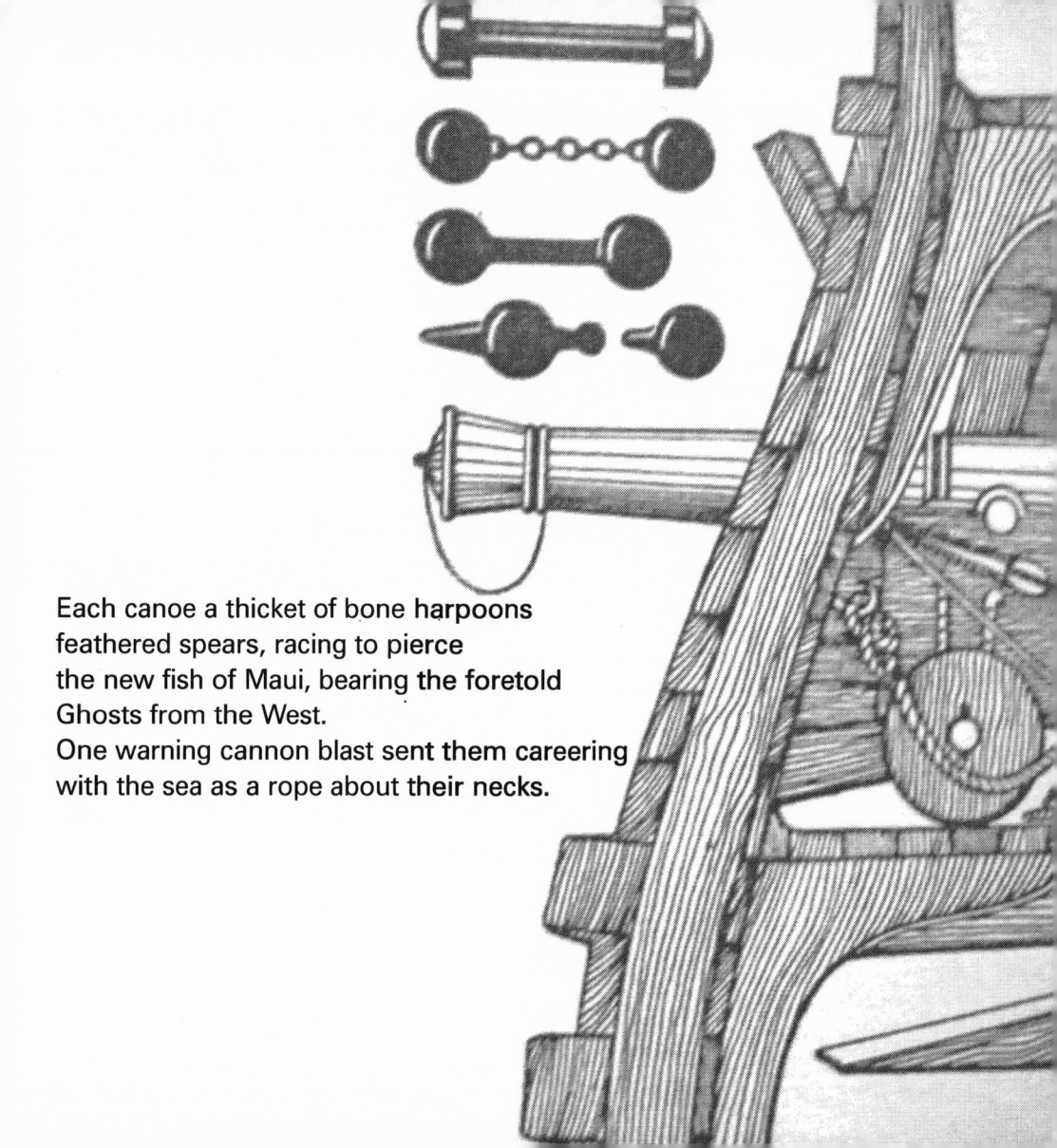

Each canoe a thicket of bone harpoons
feathered spears, racing to pierce
the new fish of Maui, bearing the foretold
Ghosts from the West.
One warning cannon blast sent them careering
with the sea as a rope about their necks.

Cook writes his journal
alone on the poop in the shade
every day between noon and one.
Then again, as dusk pours

from the vulva of waves
by tallow light he scratches paper
with his quill, dips the nip in ink
writes on, in wig and brass.

Consults charts, reads stars
makes lunar calculations. Here his word
is Law. We cling to the few he gives us
as there's nowt else to cling to at all.

Later Mr Hicks, Mr Gore and Mr Banks,
the scientists and their artists dine
to agree a course that'll lead us on in spirals
till we end where once we started.

I'll be back in the flesh before you know it.
Meantime, Dearest, make do with me spirit.
For it flew homing, months back, must be
rounding the Cape of Good Hope, by now.

Heading for the eaves of Arguments Yard
where you'll be curing herring for the stalls;
singing the bairns to sleep, or clipping
the buggers round the ear for their cheek.

And I write my own script
between waking and sleeping
from my swinging hammock, from the yardarm
to the ship's endless hymn of creaks.

I write it in the air with a fingertip
on clouds for paper that start to shred
before my spittle-ink is dry.

My journal tells another tale than Cook's
though we share the self-same route;
out from the margins of knowingness
where we give our names to dragons.

Young Nick's Head, Poverty Bay
Cape Flattery, The Savage Isles
Cape Farewell, Point Rodney
Cook Straight, Cape Runaway.

It seems I've run as far as any man can.

We are so far from home
that hearth and kin
the ways of the town house
the bristling streets onto Market Place
the steaming stench of stables
horse shoes on Ayton Green
drumming the moorland into dales
church bells chiming behind harbour walls
the carriage rides to quay-side bars
a'swill wi' bellows, giggles and a fiddle's song
then on to the smuggling hold
in Dark Entries Yard
where Mister Ross caught us
cracked his head on a cornerstone
where you stood like an iceberg
before turning to run
both of us knowing the Hellish thing we'd done
and me saying; 'Get up Albert. Get up, Man,'
then the call of the press gang
drift by each night like whale song in sea-fog.
I'm afraid if I reach England, I'll see right through her.
Sail right on through her. I'll not be leaving again.

We pick our way north along an unending coastline
of shallow straights, keys and coral reefs
with the eyes straight from my childhood dreams
watching from the beaches; as rocks, as trees.

As sea-ribbed sand and shade. Their bodies painted
the rarest colours, in patterned dots, in perfect smears
in prints of light; these lizard men and butterfly maids;
perch and hover on the verge of a burning forest.

They point to our utter strangeness, dismiss us as a vision;
one of those floating islands full of tree climbing bears.

A bad idea, that'll repeat on them.

They stick their heads in the sand
turning back to standing stones and driftwood.
The sky blistering over a landmass we daren't acknowledge
lest it swallow us whole like the telescopic stare of a Cyclops
and like the big crocs we bait with fish.

Steering through shoals and sand banks
at a distance of 2 or 3 leagues from the shore.
20 fathom. 4 fathom. 21 fathom. 11 and 18 fathom.
8, 12 and 10 fathom. Very irregular ground.

Disaster bites like the great white shark
Mr Banks sketched last week.

Timbers crunch in twilight.
The Endeavour pig-squeals.
We find ourselves gutted on the edge of a reef.
She is gulping gallons of this turquoise sea.

All our efforts 'll not break her free.
The pumps are churning. We scramble with poles
and ropes, yell and blow to lever her off
the spine that's punched a hole through the hull.

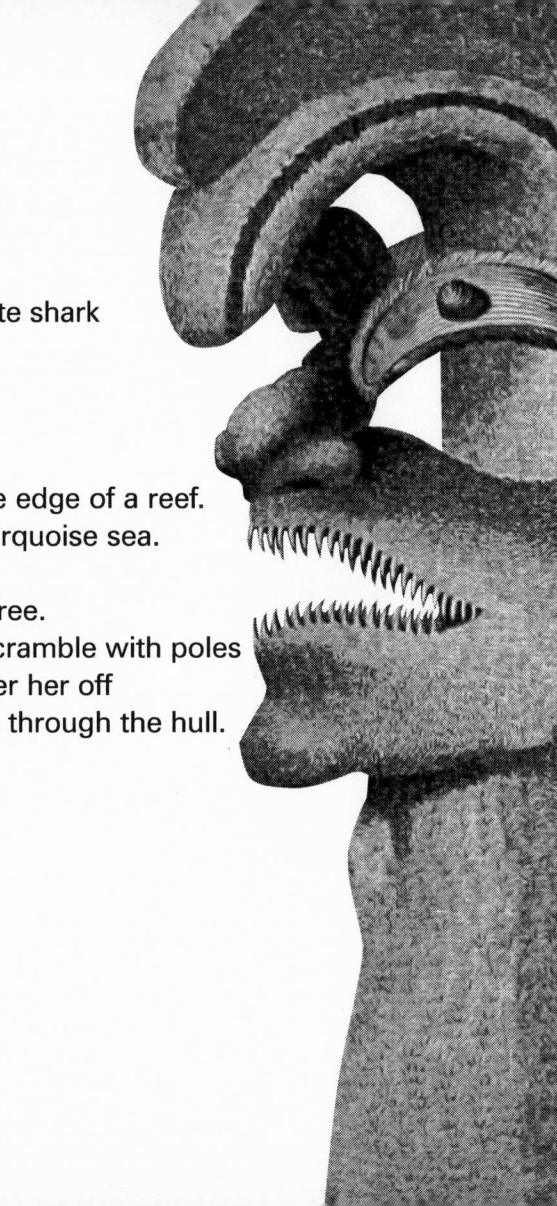

We dump the big guns and the ballast to keep her afloat.
She's pitching like a pierced sow with each battering swell.
The masters calling '…fall to 't yearly, we've run ourselves aground.
Lower the longboats and the yawl or she'll drag us down to he

But we are determined bears who remember being men.

The hole is plugged with white coralled bone;
we circle the ship with soundings, bail, pump
grapple sheer luck, stretch a sail-dressing over the leak
till the next full tide takes us limping on.

The sea a slipknot about our necks.

Beached in venomous gales
in an inlet of slime and silt.
When it is not rain, it's the vapours
both of which scald the eyes and throat.
The air is a thick insect soup.

Work goes on to repair the ship.
We reap what we can from the bush.
Make rope. Split wood. Forge nails
and bolts. Recaulk the hull.

Around the camp we erect
Carpentaria's first monstrous fence.
One by one men fall ill.

Mr Banks, Solander, and Monkhouse
(the ship's Doctor among 'em).
Even Tayeto and Tupia, our angels
from Neverland. Dr Monkhouse
will be the first to die of the fever.

Cook 'll not have us drinking the waters
as they're libel to send you mad.
Our skins crawl with stings and sores.
The stinking jungles bellow and thrash.

While nightime swells with coughs then shrieks
each morning the Sun rides up from the East
to be shredded at sight by a flock of red parakeets

shoaling to squabble over it like the Prince Bishop's banquet
laid-out across the canopy where its scavenged by monkeys

dropping red flakes of the morning
as fire-flower blossom
into the foaming mouths of the delta.

Light like that never reaches far into mangroves.

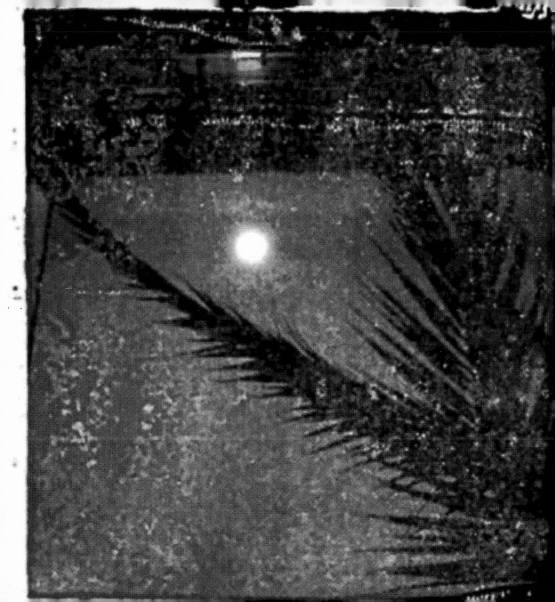

We keep our death fires burning
the water pots boiling.

A party of marines left at noon
to scout the outback. They've not yet
returned from its weave, though since
we have heard no gunshots
nor any human cries.

There are sets of footprints on the South river sandbank.
The smudge of a campfire a league further on
and smooks in the woods all down the shore.

We have feasted on turtles, fish and a kangaroo.
While the monkeys danced a funerary rite
the cockatoo sobbed lamentations
that turn bears and men into roasting swine.

We watch the bush for signs of cannibals
strain our ears for yidaki drones
dread a mound of familiar faces
neatly stuffed with herbs.

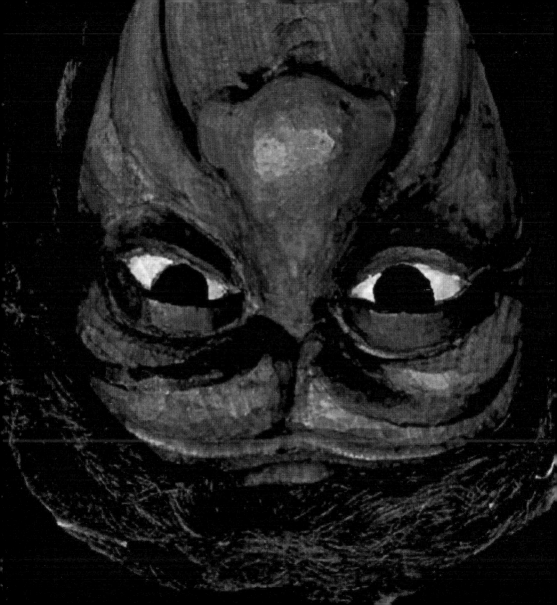

Dusk, and the men are still missing.
The nightly forests start to grind.
Bats spew from ground pits, hunting
fireflies between the trunks and beyond
in a black river called Fur or Leather or Hunger.

Wander out of the camp's makeshift fence
and the mat will take you to make a cliff
from your brow, cast gullies with your sinews;
it may craft a red hill from your heart.

I toss my lost tooth into the river
called Fur or Leather or Hunger;
see it bounce, tumble, start to howl,
grow paws, ears, a lolling tongue, a tail
and hind leg, lifted to scent the dog fence
before it darts along my tendons
pounding out the Emu trails.

Ravenhill and Jacob had us toast Old Jove
sailing over the bell of the bay in exile
Singing; This yar neet,, this yar neet
              Every neet 'an all
              Ti Whinny Moor thoo cums at last
til we're emersed in the cusp of the Thunder Moon.

The same Emersion happened at Greenwich
according to calculation on the 30th at 5h17'43"
in the P.M: the difference is 14h18'50" of Longitude
which this place is west of Greenwich.

The Captain keeps to the officer's tent
until he's due to take his rounds.
Gives praise and thanks, then visits the sick.

There's been bickering among the Gentlemen
over the missing marines. He is loath to send
any more into the matt as we've scarce
enough hands for the ship once she's well.

Our skeleton ship is about ready to sail.
The carpenters agree she's seaworthy;
close enough to land us in New Guinea.

Young Jacob Howe died shivering
as Cook made the final assessment.
Afore Christ tuk up his saul
he told me to take his Ma a knotted lock of his hair.
Venus, grant me a visit to see the Ugthorpe Witch.

Who lived all her years in the same sea-gripped cove
with the Hob, her boggarts and a bag of drowned spirits
an' I'll explain just how far her youngest reached.

Bob Beagrie was born in Middlesbrough, in 1967. He lives there with his wife and daughter and works as a freelance in schools and with community groups. He is a founding member of an experimental arts collective Heterogloss; responsible for a range of arty-facts including video pieces, artists bookworks, and permanent and temporary installations. He worked as Literature Officer for Cleveland Arts for five years and co-ran The Verb Garden, a live literature event. In 2002 he won the Biscuit Poetry Prize and in March 2003 he was presented with a Northern Writers Time to Write Award, funded by The Northern Rock Foundation. He has performed at venues across the country and in Europe.

by the same author

Huginn & Munnin, Biscuit Publishing Ltd (2002)

Masque: The Art of the Vampyre, Mudfog (2001)

Bus Shelter Observations, Heterogloss (1996)

Gothic Horror, Mudfog (1996)

First published 2004 by
Biscuit Publishing Ltd
PO Box 123, Washington
Newcastle upon Tyne
NE37 2YW

www.biscuitpublishing.com
info@biscuitpublishing.com

ISBN 1-903914-13-2

Photographs from live performance by
Holly Eve Watson.
Copyright 2004

Design and layout by
James Cianciaruso
Archetype
Copyright 2004
Tel:08702 245 151

www.archetype-uk.com